A Memoir of India
1942–1946

A Memoir of India
1942–1946

Gerald Elliot

First published in 2014 by Gerald Elliot

ISBN: 978 0 9928 120 0 3

Designed and typeset by Mark Blackadder

Printed and bound in Britain by
Bell and Bain Ltd, Glasgow

Introduction

———

I first put together this Memoir of India for family and friends in 1960. I have now rewritten and expanded it for publication with the hope that it may interest a wider circle.

Gerald Elliot
November 2013

PART I

Travel and Training

———

I served in India between 1942 and 1946 as an officer in the great Indian Army of the British Empire. My service ran from August 1942 to February 1946.

My enlistment for India was not predestined. When the date for call-up, my 18th birthday, was coming close I considered the possible choices. I had no interest in the Navy, where my father had made his career as a surgeon. My school, Marlborough College in Wiltshire (MC), had good army connections, in particular with the Kings Royal Rifles, considered a cut above the excellent county regiments, but India came to attract me most. An uncle had been in the Indian Army during and after the First World War. Another uncle, brother of my father, was in the Indian Medical Service and was currently personal physician to the Viceroy, Lord Linlithgow. Another aunt was a missionary in India, carrying on the tradition of the Church of Scotland. So I signed on for India after an interview by General Lockhart, a senior officer of the Indian Army (IA).

When I returned to St Andrews in April 1942 after my last term at MC my mother found an old Indian Civil Service (ICS) officer who was ready to give me lessons in Urdu before I left for India. This was Sir Fred Johnston, who had retired twenty years previously as Governor of Baluchistan. Sir Fred provided me with a grammar and I progressed well in not more than six lessons. A simple exercise was to recount a day's activity, not forgetting my morning shit.

I left home in June 1942 to visit ex-school friends in the south and only returned for a few days in August to prepare for the voyage to India. The heavy baggage allowance was very modest, perhaps 60 lb, and I restricted my civilian kit to one outfit. As a keen violinist I resolved to find room for my instrument, despite the mockery of friends and family. Who had heard of a soldier taking his music to war? I riposted that a career in the Indian Army did not necessarily involve perpetual active service in the jungle or desert. To protect my violin from the ravages of red ants, common in Indian houses, I bought a heavy steel violin case from Beare's famous shop in Wardour Street.

Towards the end of August I reported to Redford Barracks and signed on pro-forma to the Royal Scots, with standard battle-dress uniform and a white band as an officer cadet. Tropical kit was issued, including khaki shorts with large turn-ups and the standard solar topi with long brim and neck piece. These, we found later, had already been discarded in favour of simpler topis, or even berets, and shorts without turn-ups.

Several of us cadets went straight to London, lodging in the Great Central Hotel at Marylebone. The hotel had been taken over at the beginning of the war and used as a transit camp for troops on their way abroad. The draft I joined, about a hundred strong, was mainly ex schoolboys new to military life. I was equally ignorant, apart from having been in the Corps at MC and a week of home defence training there. We were there for about a fortnight before our draft left. We were kept busy by small route marches through the centre of London, physical training on the hotel roofs and occasional lectures on India. There was also church parade on Sundays. At one lecture I was the only person to declare some slight knowledge of Urdu. A close MC friend, Kennedy McWhirter, was in the draft. I was able to enjoy his family's hospitality in their large house at Winchmore Hill, also visiting my aunt in Knightsbridge. Unfortunately when the draft moved to embark for India I was left behind, with two other cadets. I had hung out some washing to dry and it was pinched by a soldier, who was quickly found and arrested. He was court martialled within weeks. The three of us had to appear and give evidence identifying our stolen property. I wept on missing our draft. Consolation was provided by a fine Regimental Sergeant Major (RSM) retired from active service, who drilled and befriended us. When the next draft arrived at the Grand Central I was able to help with their registration and found two school mates among them.

Our draft very soon moved off. We were put on the evening train to Liverpool and embarked directly on *Capetown Castle*. This was a fine passenger liner, built shortly before the war and commandeered for troop transport. For the voyage to India she was, I think, carrying about two thousand men. We hundred cadets were housed in a large superstructure built on the main deck with three tiers of bunks. Though in cramped space they proved quite comfortable.

We left Liverpool only to anchor in Belfast Lough, where we had to wait some days for our convoy to muster. I was fortunate to draw a winning ticket to be shown round our escort, HMS *Durban*, a small cruiser. Durban was an ex WWI product of lend lease. She was lightly armed and did not impress.

When we finally started to sail south we settled into a routine. There was PT on deck every morning; we were thoroughly exercised on life saving procedures, and portholes and windows had to be masked with blackout material. Autumn 1942 was the most dangerous period for U-boat attacks. I spent my time reading and playing bridge. A welcome partner was M. A. Rahman, who was returning home fresh from St Pauls. Food was adequate, with a preponderance of fried liver. There were daily Urdu lessons. Though I had so far learnt very little, I was given a class to instruct and managed to keep a small jump ahead. One of the cadets organised a concert party and pulled me in to contribute on my violin. At the show I played two pieces very badly and was only redeemed from disgrace by moving into Scottish reels.

We arrived in Durban after about five weeks at sea. As we moved past the pier head we were greeted by the Lady Mayor of Durban in a long white dress singing Land of hope and glory. It is recorded that she greeted thus every troop ship that called at Durban during the war. She well deserved her recognition by a medal. For the citizens of Durban it was a point of honour to ensure that all troops coming ashore were looked after. I got horribly drunk one evening, though less so than my host, who collapsed and had to be put to bed by his wife.

We finally arrived in Bombay in mid December, passing the great Gateway of India. Our draft went to the Officers Training School (OTS) at Mhow, leaving the three of us destined for Bangalore. My military ignorance was shown up when I was called in by our draft commander Colonel Monier-Williams to get orders for our journey to Bangalore. I hadn't realised that unless you are a defaulter you salute and do not remove your cap.

We disembarked with our kit, dined at a Chinese restaurant, resisting the grand and unique Taj Mahal hotel, and climbed into the hard 3rd class carriage which was to take us south. Having been beaten in the competition for space to lie out we changed at the dismal junction of Guntakal, and eventually after travelling for a night and a day arrived in Bangalore.

The draft from which we had been held back had gone to the OTS in Bangalore. We were fortunately allowed to join its course although it had already completed the first month. I was reunited with McWhirter and found a new friend in Harold Holloway, ex St Pauls School. We spent much of our free time together. I was put in a different training company, composed almost entirely of Indians and Anglo Indians, as we termed them (Eurasians), with a few country-born Europeans. As British cadets we got on well with those groups. Many of the Indians were professional soldiers who had become havildars or Viceroy's Commissioned Officers (VCOs) before being put up for officer training. Others, belonging to the so styled military classes, had joined to become officers. There were a few who would never have been considered by the peace-time army, such as Bengalis and Madrasis. These, though sometimes physically delicate, became after training entirely worthy officers. Some of the Anglos, elderly by our standards, had given up their civil careers to enlist. At their age they were in particular demand for the Royal Indian Army Service Corp, commonly known as the Rice Corp. Off parade the different racial groups hardly mingled, as might be expected. But I did find a good friend in an ex Jemadar (junior officer) of the 12th Frontier Force Regiment (FFR), who tried vainly to improve my pitiful performance on the high jump. Sports were important at Bangalore. I was an indifferent performer; McWhirter excelled at the hundred yards and weight lifting. I played hockey quite well, but the British were quite outclassed by the Indians. India had already adopted the now standard light and small-headed stick and they were very quick and skilful tacklers. J. S. Maples, a MC master who arrived at Bangalore as a pre-officer training instructor, an international hockey player, was left standing.

Another MC recruit to Bangalore in our time was

Arthur Dee, who joined to run pre-training of Indian cadets. We made a habit of dining together on Saturday evenings at the West End Hotel in the town, an easy bike ride from the School area. Dee had been a friend as a master in MC days and our friendship continued after the war.

At Christmas 1942 we were all given a week's holiday. The Indian cadets no doubt went home. Many of the British took off to visit Mysore or Madras. Having only just arrived I decided with McWhirter not to travel away. For entertainment we were taken to visit the Hindustan aircraft factory, which was building small planes for the war. We were told that initially it had a reputation for crashes due to bad workmanship. This was corrected by requiring that trial flights of new planes should always include some of those directly responsible for assembling them. My 19th birthday was on Christmas Eve. I spent some of the morning on an exercise crawling through a ditch well adorned with human shit.

The training at Bangalore was intense but tolerable. There were many all-day exercises for which we were bussed up to twenty miles from the town. Towards the end there was a twenty-four hour exercise ending with a twenty mile march home, relieved by delicious mangoes. In the hotter weather we had afternoon lectures and TEWTS – Tactical Exercises Without Troops. Great effort was needed to avoid falling asleep and being put on a charge. We ran regularly over an assault course where I consistently failed to climb a high brick wall with the ropes provided. I worked hard on my Urdu with a Muslim munshi and a delightful Hindu from the north. I took the lower exam on arrival at Bangalore and followed with the higher certificate early at Abbottabad.

My health at Bangalore was normal, except for persistent jungle sores, ulcers which developed from infected scratches and were slow to heal. They stopped on my departure from

Bangalore to the cleaner north and never recurred. One of our trio of latecomers, John Taylor, was afflicted by a form of dysentery which kept him in hospital for many weeks, and he had to drop back from our course. He recovered fully and took part in the Kohima battles.

The School provided decent, mainly European, food for the British cadets – no shortage of meat, butter or bread, all rationed at home. For beer only the undrinkable Bangalore Bitter was available. Murree and Solan in the north made good stuff but it was reserved for Burma. For the equipment we would need as officers including a tin trunk we were guided to the local contractor Shamsuddin. There were frequent complaints about his prices. Some complaints, of course baseless, implied dirty work with the Commandant.

The course finished in April and we all graduated with the glory of a second lieutenant's single pip, which would be joined by a second after six months. Cadets had been invited to give their preference for postings – British cadets favoured the Gurkhas. Impressed by the reputation of Frontier Regiments I logged 13th Frontier Force Rifles (FFRif). However, several of us, including McWhirter, perhaps for supposed superior brains, were recruited for Special Intelligence though given a pro-forma posting in the regiments we chose. Holloway put down for a well-known cavalry regiment and was duly gazetted for it. But he discovered that a friend, who had put down for the same regiment in which his father, a general, had served, was instead allocated to the 3rd Madras. Holloway, with great generosity, got the postings reversed.

There was a special dinner for our passing out. I was placed beside the Chief Urdu Instructor, a Lt Colonel. He put me right on the correct pronunciation of Panjab, for which I was grateful. The Commandant of the OTS, Brigadier Jones, presided. Towards the end our senior cadet,

Tidman, proposed a toast to the Indian Army and in particular to the Indian Sepoy. We drank it. Brigadier Jones was a
bit deaf and in replying he gave the same toast; we shared it
again.

Newly commissioned officers were normally given a
week's leave before taking up their postings, but our little
group for Special Intelligence had to go direct to the Wire-
less Intelligence Centre (WIC) in Abbottabad. We made the
journey via Delhi and the Frontier Mail, changing at Taxila
for Havelian, the nearest station to Abbottabad five miles
away. After arrival we were plunged into intensive courses
on Japanese and the use and breaking of codes. After six
weeks we were given the choice to continue the training or
give up and move to the units to which we had pro-forma
postings. I enjoyed tackling Japanese but found the mathe-
matical work on codes very difficult. So I gave up. Anyway
I preferred the command of soldiers to intelligence work.
We were charged to preserve complete secrecy to the
outside on the work of the WIC and no doubt honoured
this, though its functions were well known elsewhere in
Abbottabad. McWhirter elected to stay on, with most of the
current trainees. I, with a new friend Len Millington,
reported to the FFRif Centre close by, where we were
welcomed by the centre adjutant Allan Sergeant.

I did get another offer six months later from the WIC. It
came from Colonel Harcourt, in peacetime, I think, an
Oxford teacher of Persian. He said they needed someone to
vet newspapers and other information from Iran. I told him
that I had no Persian, only Urdu. We can teach you Persian
quickly, he said. I declined the invitation, being happy at the
FFRif Centre. It also seemed absurd to me that Harcourt
etc. could or would not find an educated native Persian of
appropriate loyalty to do the job.

PART II

Abbottabad Years

India in the 1940s still basked in the late glory of Empire. Though it was clear that dissolution was not far off, outward appearances were much as they had been in Kipling's time. Following the Great Mutiny of 1857 Britain was generally accepted as the authority of government. During my service there I met no unfriendliness of any sort through being British. Indians, while increasingly demanding self-government, respected and appreciated the honesty and dedication of the Indian Civil Service and its supporting public bodies. That was surely the best tribute the Empire could have. But the price of Empire was high, requiring from many generations the best of the British middle classes.

It would be wrong to suggest that an almost family relationship existed all over British India and at all times. The frequent bouts of civil disorder from 1910 onwards show that this would be a sentimental myth. But it was true for much of India much of the time, and it held without qualification in the Indian Army.

The Indian Army, shattered by the Mutiny, had built itself up in a new form on troops raised in the Panjab which helped to quell the Mutiny. Over the years its regiments, as in every other army, had developed their individual esprit de corps, stiffened with periodic battle honours. Dogras, Muslims and Sikhs served happily together, though usually in separate companies, and there were no problems of caste or religion. VCOs, of high efficiency and standing, provided the link between the mainly European officers and the sepoys. In the 1930s a number of Indians were brought in as full officers, and this process of Indianisation was accelerated during the war. (Some Muslim officers became political leaders in Pakistan after the handing over of power in 1947.) The soldiers of the British Army, low paid and not held in high regard by their countrymen, were recruited from men who could not find jobs in civil life. The sepoys of the Indian Army were the elite of their areas. Certainly they served for pay, as loyal mercenaries, but they were also soldiers because it was an honourable calling where son often followed father in his regiment, retiring as a respected pensioner to his village. This difference was also reflected in the officers. In social background they might be considered inferior to British Army officers, but they seemed better professional soldiers, with their units in peacetime constantly engaged in active service on the north-west frontier.

It would be carrying my youthful loyalty too far to claim that the Indian Army was a better fighting organisation than the British. The Indians needed more careful training and better leadership than the more sophisticated British. When that was deficient their performance could be less than admirable, particularly when they were faced with conditions for which they were not prepared. This was shown in the retreat from Burma in 1942. The stiffening of tradition meant a lot to the fighting capacity of each Indian Regiment. The FFRif had this, and its war records were correspondingly distinguished. Among those who looked down on the IA was Churchill, who seems to have thought of it simply as a gigantic system of outdoor relief. But he was always prejudiced on India. Slim, the general who drove the Japanese out of Burma, was an IA officer.

I saw very little of the pre-war regulars. Most of them were in senior posts in the active battalions, and the Centre was mainly manned by Emergency Commissioned Officers (ECOs).The majors and senior captains would be men who had been in business (boxwalas) in Madras or Calcutta and possibly belonged to the local territorial units. They were strong individuals who had made their own way in life. Practically none of them, or of the young officers like myself who joined in those years, were on the public school side of the great educational divide. Is it just imagination to suppose that there was a greater richness and originality among them than in a similar British Army? At any rate eccentricities were not discouraged. In Abbottabad a colony of homosexuals flourished briefly. One officer insisted on sleeping in a tent on the sepoy lines 'to bridge the gap'. He was later killed with 8/13 in Burma leading the Sikh company in a brave assault on a Japanese position. All British officers were assumed to be Christians, but one at the Centre converted to Islam. The army establishment was horrified, and he was banished to be Station Staff Officer (SSO) at Attock, an important place for crossing the Indus but with undemanding military work.

The Commanding Officer (CO) during most of my time was Colonel 'Jimmy' James, ex Frontier Force Regiment (FFR), a firm and competent leader. He was succeeded by CE Morris, who had fought with FFRif 4/13 in Africa and was briefly held as a POW in Italy. The Second-in-Command (2I/C) initially was Stephen Loretz, 'Twinkle-toes', a homosexual aesthete, also a scholar of Pashtu and Urdu. He prescribed Henderson's *Life of Stonewall Jackson* as a textbook of military tactics. I failed to read it, though it had also been a favourite of a classics teacher at MC. Loretz was succeeded by Lt Colonel Pearson, colourless but with a lively and hospitable wife.

The Regimental Centre (RC), as well as being a transit station for officers on their way to and from the dozen or so active battalions, trained the sepoys needed to supply them. By 1944, when the great expansion of the army was taking place, there must have been 3,000 or so recruits under training, 100 passing out every month. Newly commissioned officers were attached to training companies for a few months to get some experience and then posted off to active battalions. But some were kept to run the recruit training, and I was one of those who stuck. This was partly because the active battalions were lucky in having relatively few officer casualties in 1943–45, and partly because the CO thought, quite rightly, that some of the newly commissioned officers were not mature enough to be pushed straight into active battalions. This was so in my case. I hadn't the physical or professional self-confidence at the age of 19 to make a good officer on active service. But I was far beyond most of my contemporaries in my knowledge of Urdu, so found less difficulty in the detailed administrative work needed for training soldiers.

There was a myth in the Indian Army that only certain Indian peoples made good soldiers, and an introductory pamphlet listed the qualities of each people, rather like a description of breeds of dog. Gurkhas were 'fearless', 'with a great sense of humour', Sikhs 'clever but intriguing', and so on. This view had no historic foundation, since the old Bengal and Madras armies of before the Mutiny were recruited from quite different people. In fact the Hazarawals, Gujars, Tamils, etc. who came into the army during the war acquitted themselves well, despite their lack of military background. Some were not so successful. At one point I had on my hands a bunch of Ahirs, tough ugly peasants from near Agra, who had been sent for infantry retraining after a near mutiny in the artillery. Several complained that they had been underpaid on transfer to our centre. I found that there had been such mistakes and I got them corrected. Where there were none this had to be patiently explained, though dissatisfaction remained. They seemed to be reasonably happy when they left me, but I heard later that they mutinied again in the next unit. These people must also have had a 'great sense of humour'. My aunt Mary lived as a missionary in Khurja in the middle of the Ahir country. She told me that on occasions when she was travelling round the villages and pitched her tent at night mischievous Ahirs would knock down the irrigation dykes and flood her out.

At the Centre I was put into D Battalion (Bn) one of the four large training units. I joined as a Company Officer of 8 coy. I fairly quickly became Company Commander, getting promotion to Captain in October 1944. I stayed with 8 coy until the end of the Japanese war and beyond it until it was disbanded in October 1945.

Abbottabad, a semi hill station at 3,000ft, had an ideal climate. There was some frost and snow in winter and the temperature could go into the nineties in summer just before the monsoon, with accompanying 'prickly heat', but neither extreme was troublesome. The sun shone most of the time and the weather rarely interfered with work. Offices were kept cool in summer by electric fans, or more usually pankahwalas, small boys taken on to circulate the air by working hanging pankahs (fans). They dozed in the heat on a bench outside and used their toes for the pankah cords.

I spent 30 months in Abbottabad training sepoys, a continuous spell broken only by occasional four or six week training courses in other parts of India. It was a peaceful but strenuous existence. We worked hard and with enthusiasm to turn Indian villagers into good sepoys. By that stage in the war the enormous demands for manpower to expand the army had almost exhausted the areas of normal supply. Recruiting teams combed the Panjab offering money and glory to new recruits. Retired subedars in the villages added their weight, anticipating rewards from the government in the shape of medals or land grants. But there were few left to come forward. Those remaining were too young or had to keep the farm or were unfit. Some of those were bought along by eager recruiters, who got 10 rupees a head, and even passed by recruiting officers. They then caused endless bother in the training units, as for a long time army regulations provided no way of getting rid of them. Most of the recruits came from areas and villages which had not previously supported the army. It was difficult for them to change from the free and easy life of a village peasant to the army. A number of them regretted it and there were some desertions, particularly among those who lived in the Hazara hills around Abbottabad. Fortunately for the standard of the army these deserters usually remained untraced by the local police. Either they arranged to be not at home when the constable called, or a suitable sum of money changed hands. On one occasion an English missionary appeared in Abbottabad and came to my office. 'I want my boy back' she said referring to a newly enlisted recruit, who she claimed was training as a Christian in her mission. 'Sorry;' I said, 'he has signed up for the duration of hostilities and a year afterwards. There is no provision for early discharge.' 'I won't leave without him' she said. Eventually I realised we were defeated and sent her over to the adjutant, who somehow managed to remove the boy's name from the army rolls. She departed in triumph, taking with her a very unwilling jawan (soldier).

On another occasion I felt so annoyed about the desertion of a Panjab Muslim (PM) recruit that I took a truck with a Jemadar to look for him in his village. It was predictably a useless exercise; his family declared stoutly that he had not been back to his home. It would be too much to expect villagers to deny protection to their own kind.

In the six-month training course we taught these lads to

drill and shoot. We also fed them up and made them physically fit. I had been naturally antipathetic to the 'square
bashing' army tradition, but soon came to see that an uned-
ucated group of Indian villagers could only be made into a
fighting unit if it was highly disciplined to carry out routine
actions instinctively and obey orders automatically. Drill gave
them this discipline, and created the collective pride which
a military body must have. So parade ground drill was rightly
one of the keystones of our training and in the early stages
dusty hours were spent on the parade grounds. Later the
scene shifted to the firing ranges, where each man learnt to
fire accurately at up to 500 yards. There was fortunately more
training to come, a further two months at Kakul, outside
Abbottabad, and several months of jungle training at Chindwara in CP (Central Provinces). Our training was little more
than preliminary conditioning and our sepoys needed far
more to fit them for taking on the Japs in Burma.

Apart from the disciplinary side there was a fair element
of education in our sepoy training. Few of them were literate
when they arrived and they spent many classroom hours on
reading and writing, current affairs and civics. The last two
subjects looked better on paper than they were in fact. Most
recruits had very little idea about what the war was about
and who the Japanese were anyway. They tried to remember
what was told to them, but it didn't stick. They knew that
for 30 rupees a month they had to be soldiers and fight the
enemy. This was enough. 'Civics' contained a lot of useful
information on how to make themselves more prosperous
in their villages. It was part of the programme known in
English rather pompously as 'Rural Uplift' (the Urdu was
less pretentious) which was launched shortly before the war
in the Panjab by FL Brayne of the Indian Civil Service. It
was not the sort of venture to attract much political backing
from above in peacetime but when the war came the

Government became more enthusiastic and it was introduced into army education. In essence it preached self-help
in the village, careful spending of money, use of better seed,
cleanliness, co-operative work in planting trees and digging
wells, etc., just the programme which the Indian Government still promotes. We were all enthusiastic about it, but I
doubt if our lectures, pictures and demonstrations achieved
anything. Indian peasants do not absorb knowledge and
apply it like British university students. In practice the Indian
Government has only managed to introduce these reforms
by sending skilled people in to the fields to show the villagers
over a period of time that the ideas work. Even then the
impetus often disappears when the outsider is withdrawn.
Still, though much of the educational work must have been
wasted, the army was a great civilising influence. It gave to
hundreds of thousands of Indian peasants a disciplined training, some education and an idea of what went on in the
world outside the little community where they and their
ancestors had lived for centuries.

D Bn Commander for most of my time was Bob
Hargraves. He had been a textile company manager in
Madras and joined the 2/13. He came to Abbottabad after
hard service in the Arakan broken by severe malaria.
Mepacrin had not yet become the standard anti-malaria
drug. Hargraves was very efficient, demanding and bad
tempered. We became good friends and maintained our
friendship in England after the war. I met and admired his
young wife Eve. He brought her to Abbottabad and they
settled in a nice house within the Lines.

Hargraves was ambivalent about Indians. Apart from
those with whom he worked in the Indian Army and civilian life, he generally despised them. In European company
he had no scruples about dismissing them as 'Wogs'; 'one of
our black brethren' was a favourite phrase. This prejudice

extended to most Anglo-Indians – 'touch of the tar-brush'. His attitude attracted no sympathy from British officers in the messes in Abbottabad. We saw the Indians as entirely equal colleagues. We did have a separate social life, in which the Indian officers did not care to take part, no doubt judging that as a minority they would not be welcome.

My closest companion in the early Abbottabad days was Len Millington, who was assigned to 7 Company. He departed in early 1944 to the 8/13 and quickly distinguished himself in Burma, winning a Military Cross. He came back to base on leave later in the year. I was a bit embarrassed, by then wearing three pips, that he was still a two-pipper. That was remedied shortly after. My best friend subsequently was Clifford Pinfold. He started in 7 Company in D Bn, later moving to E Bn. At first we lodged in simple frame huts, comfortable though without electricity. Then we moved to part of a house higher up the hill which John Parks, the Centre Assistant Quarter Master, had leased. Our section had electricity, provided separate bedrooms and an excellent living room with an open fireplace fired by coal. The bathroom was traditional, with a hip bath filled with hot water every evening. Shitting was into a square pot, emptied regularly by the sweeper (Mehta/Jemadar). Jemadar has now become the standard term, a minor politeness for the low-caste Hindus who fill the office. Correspondingly it has been discarded as a title for the VCOs. These are classed as junior Subedars.

Pinfold and I moved to the Parks bungalow shortly before going on leave in autumn 1944. I had bought in the bazaar a fine Aladdin paraffin lamp, silent and no less bright than the Tilley pressure lamp standard for non-electric huts. Unfortunately it fell as we were moving and the glass funnel smashed. I tried to find a replacement funnel in the town, but failed. That didn't matter since the Parks bungalow had full electricity and nothing else was needed except in occasional power cuts.

Another friend in D Bn was Peter Lugg. He had been an indigo planter before the war. Having joined 5/13th he went with the regiment to Iraq and Persia. It spent most of the war there guarding the oil fields and keeping the peace. Peter having been a major in Persia came home to the Centre to command 7 Company, reverting to Captain. With the same status as myself he was greatly superior in military knowledge and experience and his wisdom was invaluable. He was very good at cooling Hargraves in his frequent outbursts of bad temper. Peter had become very frustrated with the regiment's passive role in Persia, well away from the war fronts. Its CO made strong appeals to be relieved and sent to the war, without success until early 1945, when the regiment was moved to join the campaign in Italy. It arrived in Italy only shortly before the end of the German war, so had no service there. It then returned to Campbellpur just in time for the Japanese surrender in August 1945.

5/13th was commonly spoken of as the dasturi 'custom-keeping' paltan (regiment) for its code of strict military discipline and formality. I respected this from outside. A comrade at the Centre had rebelled against the code from inside and been returned from 5/13th in disgrace. Encouraged by Peter Lugg I maintained my interest in the regiment and might have joined it if the end of the German war and my prospective early release had not forestalled that. However, not everyone shared my ignorant enthusiasm. Twenty years after the war ended, I came to know Pat Patullo, a Harvard academic who had served in 5/13th. He told me that he had been most unhappy there. The officers who had been pre-war regulars despised the ECOs and would not mix with them socially. They were particularly down on Patullo as an American. These attitudes would no doubt have been

Above. Officers' Mess, Abbottabad, 1943

Left. D Battalion sports prizes, Abbottabad, 1945

Right. Sepoy Ali Haider, VC, Abbottabad, 1945

Below. Digging the new parade ground, Abbottabad, 1945

The author with Hank Howlett, Abbottabad, 1945

Centre officers' farewell to Col. James, Abbottabad, 1945

MELARAM

D Battalion staff, Abbottabad, 1945

The author at Dal Lake, Srinagar, 1945

quickly discarded in fighting service, but that chance never came. 5/13th were almost unique in hanging on to its cadre of regulars. Other regiments had by the end of the war become staffed almost entirely by ECOs, though keeping a regular as a CO.

The VCOs of D Bn were men with long service and experience, fully capable of commanding troops on active service as well as training units. Promotion had come mainly from seniority before the war but merit had now taken over. Our Bn Subedar Major when I joined was Labh Singh, a veteran of the 1914–18 war, followed by Kanshi Ram. VCOs were always addressed as Sahib; they addressed Kings Commissioned Officers (KCOs) likewise, deferring formally to the higher status, though junior KCOs with little experience and often scant knowledge of Urdu could not do other than follow the guidance of their VCOs.

I worked closely with my company Dogra Subedar, Shankar Singh, until a day when the CO Col. James, making a surprise visit to our Lines, caught him gossiping with a fellow VCO when he should have been with his recruits, and demoted him to Jemadar on the spot. His replacement was another Dogra, Durga, a figure of quiet dignity and authority. The best of my Jemadars was Kamal Khan, very competent in organising and looking after our young recruits. He was more a father than a chastiser of his flock. When a jawan was bought to him for some offence, Kamal Khan rather than punishing him would appeal to his better nature and chide him for letting down his friends, his training group, his company or the army. Such treatment often worked, with no further action needed.

I became friendly with a Sikh Jemadar, Channan Singh, who spent a few months in D Bn before being posted to 6/13th on active service in Italy. He spoke good English, though we always conversed in Urdu. 6/13th returned to

India in 1945 after hard campaigning in Italy and marched triumphantly through Abbottabad with its recent VC, Ali Haider. Channan Singh led his platoon and we resumed our friendship. I heard nothing of his subsequent career. He was no doubt quickly commissioned and reached high rank in the post-war Indian Army.

We usually had a route march of one or other recruit groups once a week as part of its training. I took them off into the hills around town, where we followed winding foot-paths over the ridges and down into narrow valleys with clumps of pine trees and remote villages beside tumbling streams. In summer there was one favourite route to a spot called Thanda Pani (cold water) halfway up to the highest mountain in the district, Thandiani. There a river made great deep pools of cool water and we all stripped and went in. In the level places in the valleys the villagers grew maize which, unless checked, the sepoys would pillage as they marched past, as they liked corn cobs for supper.

My company's parade ground was a flattened expanse above the Lines and at the foot of the round green hills which flank Abbottabad. At each side there was a deep nala, eroded by the monsoon rains, and the two nalas joined each other below it. To get to the ground you had to scramble into the nala depth and up again, but once there you were safe from surprise. The approach of a senior officer on the far side of the nala could be spotted, and this gave time for matters to be tidied up before his arrival. But there was no shade on the ground and this was tiresome in mid-summer when the temperature could go up into the nineties. I planted four trees up there and tended them lovingly. I hope that they still survive, and that I was able to leave behind one small contribution to India's welfare.

Apart from the route marches I used to spend the first two hours or so of the day on parade, and the rest of the time in and about the office on various administrative jobs. There were training programmes to be made out, stores to be checked and issued, justice of a sort to be dispensed and a lot of paper work. In retrospect much of this must have been unnecessary. There was a basic document which every recruit had to have, called a sheet-roll. This was prepared in his training battalion, was filled in with his military history and passed through his military life with him. Most of the entries and all corrections had to be initialled by an officer. We spent hours going through sheet-rolls checking and initialling routine clerical entries. There were also payroll accounts, which should have been left to havildar clerks, but had to be rechecked to avoid disastrous errors that gave 30 rupees too much to Rup Chand and the same too little to Lal Singh.

In retrospect we were less critical than we should have been of this mass of paper. We were proud of the Indian Army and our own companies. We were conscientious and enthusiastic, ready to work long hours six and seven days a week, skimping meals and rejecting afternoon swims and tennis at the Abbottabad Club. We were sarcastic about the paperwork but accepted it as an inevitable part of the package deal. We did wage war against 'bullshit', the cultivation of appearances for their own sake to impress senior officers. We (Cliff Pinfold and myself) fought continually with our adjutant, who had time on his hands and spent it devising schemes for beautifying our Lines or the layout of equipment for inspection. Fortunately our battalion commander, though often tiresome, saw through them and was usually on our side. This window dressing seemed a ludicrous distortion of values diverting everyone's energies from what was of real importance.

I saw all too little of the Hazara countryside. We were worked hard with only Sundays free, so there were no weekends to allow exploring. I had only two spells in the country near Abbottabad, one just after I arrived, the other just before I left. A few days after arrival and still entirely ignorant of my role as an officer I was sent out to umpire in a brigade 'scheme' in the hills towards the Black Mountains. We climbed up and down in fearful heat led by an ancient colonel who had done this all his life and showed no signs of stress when the rest of us were all in. At night we camped under the stars and the mess table was made by digging two parallel trenches into which we put our legs. My only contribution as an umpire was reporting that a 3 inch mortar which I inspected had been wrongly set up. This was indignantly rubbished by the officer responsible. I remember that scheme particularly because when we were marching back we passed, in a section of Panjabi sepoys, the most beautiful person I have ever seen, so dazzling that I could not take my eyes off him and turned back to look again after we had passed. He probably came from Hazara, where light skins and fine features were common.

The second escape to the mountains was at Shinkiari in 1946. I was in idleness, waiting for my release to come through. There was a camp up in the pine trees an hour's drive to the north. The army had given it up but the tents and stores had to be looked after. So I went up there with a fledgling British officer from the Centre and a company of garrison sepoys, middle-aged worthies who could not go on active service. (I suspect that most of them were well under 45; but they all seemed, and many were, doddering greybeards. Age comes quickly under the Indian sun.) We amused ourselves marching through the pines to the bare tops of the hills, an exercise which the garrison men did not like. We went dog shooting and wiped out the motley herd of dogs which had lived on the camp in its days of prosperity and still hung around the kitchen. In the evening I taught myself the foxtrot and waltz with the gramophone playing and Victor Sylvester's admirable book in my hand. It was a lovely spot and would have made an admirable TB sanatorium – in fact I think there was one a few miles down the road. Eventually we took down the tents, packed up everything and abandoned the place. The morning of our departure we found that some groundsheets had disappeared. After an hour of frantic search, the local tehsildar presented himself and reported that he had found them in a nala close to the camp. In gratitude I wrote him a rosy testimonial. The subedar suspected that the operation had been organised throughout by the tehsildar with this object. He was probably right.

Young officers were often sent on specialist courses before being posted to active battalions and I followed the same route, though keeping my stable job at the Centre in command of 8 coy. My first course was Driving and Maintenance (D&M), six weeks at Arangaon near Ahmednagar. That involved driving 15cwt and 3 ton trucks, learning the basic lore of engine maintenance, and mastering motor cycles. I was nominated for a much more demanding Motor Transport Officers (MTO) course less than two months later. A dozen of us were allotted to a skilled Staff Sergeant who had been a mechanic in civilian life. We spent the first week working with tools to make a spanner out of a chunk of steel. I was a hopeless tool maker, particularly incompetent in the slow business of filing the very hard metal into its proper shape. Although I managed a decent grade from the course I showed up as far too low in manual dexterity to make an efficient MTO. I hope the course organisers reported that to my Centre.

During the D&M course I was able to visit my school friend Sam Fitze. He had followed me to India a year later and was a cadet at the Army Fighting Vehicle School (AFV) at Ahmednagar. He had become the senior cadet of his course and was shortly to pass out to join the 19th Lancers. He arranged for me to join the farewell party and dance. There were few women in Ahmednagar to provide partners but he had found a suitable girl, possibly the sister of a fellow cadet. On the evening of the party we went by tonga to pick her up from her home. She emerged, a pretty, light-skinned 16 year old, and we were introduced to her mother, moderately brown, and her grandmother, very dark. The party was cheerful and we delivered the girl safely home at the end of it. At the end of my MTO course I was able to spend a Sunday with my brother Ian at Deolali where he was a cadet training for the Indian Artillery. We swam happily in a large lake outside the town. While waiting for the train for Bombay I heard from the station master of a huge explosion there. Two ammunition-carrying ships had collided in the harbour and blown up, killing several hundred people and destroying many buildings. I saw the full extent of the damage in Bombay.

That was the only time I coincided with Ian in India. He was commissioned into the Indian Army as a gunner and served in Burma and Java, where our troops were assailed by nationalist units determined not to allow the Dutch back into Indonesia. He was demobbed and returned home a year after me. When recounting his fighting experiences in Java he named a favourite colleague in his battery, Captain Seshaudri, and I told him that Seshaudri had become a friend of mine when we shared a tent on my first D&M course.

I took a further course in Abbottabad during the summer of 1944. This was a general course for young officers, training them not only in current tactics for battle but also in administration, staff work, culture and history. The participants were drawn from various regimental centres in the north as well as our own. The course leader was Major General R. D.

Inskip CB CIE DSO MC, a splendid man. He had fought with the 59th regiment (6/13) in the first war, and progressed from there to command the North Western Area. Though now considered too old for active service he ran these courses with immense vigour and competence. Our activities combined field activities, lectures and studies. At the end of each day we had to write up all we had learnt, this requiring at least two hours' work. One of our lectures came from a Gurkha colonel. He spoke of the history of the Gurkhas and ended with an emotional and moving passage written by a Gurkha General, Richard Turner. General Inskip also brought in an Indian scholar of some distinction for a lecture on Indo–British relationships. He, though clearly a strong anglophile, deplored how in the 20th century relations had worsened. Indians had admired and respected the British in the times of Queen Victoria, 'The Great Queen'; but in the following decades the British had distanced themselves and become unfriendly and arrogant. The lecture was in English but General Inskip ruled that questions and answers would be in Urdu. I, almost alone of my course, was ready to air my language knowledge. I made an idiomatic comment suggesting that this decline in cordiality was less due to British attitudes than to the growth of Indian nationalist feeling. The lecturer noted my reservation but did not modify his own judgement. General Inskip was friendly to me as an enthusiastic member of his course. One day I was afflicted with a severe and persistent headache. He noticed this and sent me straight to hospital where I was kept for a couple of days. Aspirin had no effect, but the doctor diagnosed my trouble as blocked sinuses. This quickly cleared up through breathing camomile steam and I returned to my course.

There was only one other time when I had to look to a doctor in Abbottabad. I was putting a bunch of recruits through gas drill. They were taken into a hut with their gas masks on and exposed to tear gas from canisters. When we were satisfied that the masks were working properly they had to remove them and stand for a few moments breathing tear gas. I did the same. Shortly afterwards a fierce rash came out on my body and I went over to our doctor, Baij Nath, at the Centre. He was undisturbed, telling me that it would soon go away, as it did.

I was sent on a Battle Course in Dehra Dun towards the end of 1944. I was reluctant to go as I was working hard on my Urdu in preparation to sit for an interpretership. I tried with the Centre adjutant Allan Sergeant to be excused from it, but he was adamant. The Centre had been charged to provide an officer and I was the only suitable person available. Training for war took precedence over academic studies. The Battle Course turned out to be of good value, a mixture of tactical instruction and strenuous but not punishing exercises in the belt of forest around Dehra Dun. I managed to get a decent grade, though I failed to secure from ambush a fighting patrol which I was leading. On another full-day exercise my party mistook its position and had to make a long extra climb up one of the forest hills. Doubling out of the forest at the end of one exercise I fell and twisted my ankle badly. I limped painfully for the rest of the course. I discovered from a Border Regiment officer on my course that my first cousin, Gavin Elliot, also from the Borders Regiment, was in Dehra Dun on a Senior Officers Course. I knew him slightly but we had not met for years. He was now second in command in his battalion, preparing to go into Burma. I visited him in his tent and enjoyed dinner in his mess.

After the Dehra Dun Battle Course I was allowed a straight run at the Centre studying for the Urdu interpretership exam. I worked on this most of the time between coming off parade and dinner. I crammed hard to broaden my vocabulary and to understand the prescribed Urdu literature. Reading manuscripts was necessary but difficult; the form of the lettering often varied from standard print. The exam was held in Lahore in June. I stayed in the 8th Punjab Centre and was able to attend an Old Marlburian (OM) Dinner at the Punjab Club with 15 OMs present, mainly older than myself. A month later the exam results came through and I found myself an Interpreter, First Class. Winning the top grade was quite unjustifiable; my knowledge was very superficial. It is possible that the examiners wanted to give special encouragement to ECOs. I shed much of my literary acquisitions pretty quickly, though my colloquial ability has remained, strengthened by many return visits to India for business and as a tourist. The news came from the Centre office at the end of a day of Battalion sports. I was very depressed on the defeat of 8 coy by 7 coy, which had reversed our initial lead by successes in the running events. I cheered up and we had a small celebration at dinner in the mess. The reward for a First Class Interpretership was 1,400 rupees, two months' pay. Part, according to custom, went to my munshi, and I had already bought for 200 rupees a wind-up gramophone and ten records or so. Cliff Pinfold and I got great pleasure from this, though on some of the 12-inch records it wound down before it got to the end and had to be boosted. After Urdu I started on Panjabi, but the stimulus of a goal had gone, and I didn't learn much. One Saturday when I was leading a group on a twelve-mile route march the Jemadar, part of whose job was to stiffen and encourage any lagging jawans, came up and told me that we were passing close to the home village of one of our recruits. Could we give him leave for an hour or two to visit his family. This was quite irregular, but I accepted the plea and even re-routed our march to pass the jawan's village, where I was offered and accepted a refreshment of tea.

My bearer throughout my time was Zain Khan from the village of Nawanshahr, two miles outside Abbottabad. When Len Millington and I selected bearers on our arrival at the Centre in 1943 I favoured a flamboyant and good looking candidate but Millington grabbed him first. He turned out to be unreliable and dishonest. My alternative choice Zain Khan proved entirely satisfactory, honest and loyal, ready to work all hours. Officers' bearers were required to be present in the Mess to wait on their Sahibs at lunch and sometimes dinner. He did this faithfully, only complaining if I came back from the Lines excessively late for lunch or not at all.

He gave special help on one occasion. The jawans took bayonets of the small stabbing design with them on route marches. One day on the return of a group from its march three bayonets were found to be missing. There was a great furore. Had they been secretly passed to tribesmen, who might have welcomed an addition to their armoury? There was no evidence of this and it appeared that they had not been properly fixed in belts and had fallen out. A search party was sent out on the Nawanshahr road and found one of the missing three lying there. Zain Khan himself made an extra journey to his village and was handed a second bayonet which had been picked up; the third was given up for lost. Zain Khan supervised the works of other menials, the bhisti (water carrier) and sweeper, in my case a humble woman. He shopped for me in the bazaar and looked after my clothes and kit. One valuable acquisition was a canvas water bag (chaghal) which he inscribed with his own name, not mine. I still have it. Zain Khan had a young family for which he was the sole provider. He brought them in once to visit me. I paid him off well when I left in February 1946. We corresponded once or twice and I sent him a little money to help.

I only once took part in a Court Martial in India. The victim was a Sikh sepoy who had been given leave prior to transfer to the jungle training centre at Chindwara and had not returned. He was quickly picked up by the military police and charged for desertion. I studied the manual of Indian Military Law to get the relevant entry. The wording for a charge sheet read somewhat as follows: Sepoy Surjan Singh (an example) at Abbottabad, while on active service, deserted the colours, failing to return from leave on the due date or after. Another formulation would specifically cover mutiny: Surjan Singh declared 'you may do what you will. I will soldier no more.' The Court had to consist of commissioned officers, and there was provision for an officer or VCO to attend and argue the case for the accused. As a member of the Court I was impressed by the case for the defence. When the verdict had to be decided, I as the most junior member had to vote first. My verdict was absent without leave, not desertion. But my colleagues all found this a clear case of desertion; no doubt with more experience I would have agreed with them.

I had three periods of leave during my time in India. I was unable in April 1943 to take the week joining leave normally given to new officers. The several of us posted to the WIC in Abbottabad were required to report there immediately. Having settled at FFRif Centre I was able to take my deferred right in October with a trip to Delhi, staying with my uncle Henry Elliot. Henry, a colonel in the Indian Medical Service (IMS), was then the personal physician of the Viceroy Lord Linlithgow, a post of great distinction. He had an interesting career behind him, including as doctor to the British Embassy at Kabul. Apart from his personal qualities he may well have been favoured through being a bachelor. His tenure in Delhi coincided with Linlithgow as Viceroy. He retired from the IMS about a year before independence. Before retiring to the UK he was invited to join the famous naturalist George Sheriff in a plant hunting trip to Tibet. They brought back to Edinburgh a new rhododendron and were recognised in its labelling.

Uncle Henry had his own house on the Viceroy's estate, designed by Edwin Lutyens, the great architect of New Delhi, and I stayed comfortably there. My friends from WIC Abbottabad were still training at the larger centre in Delhi and we were able to use the Viceregal facilities for swimming and tennis. Uncle Henry took me round the grand Viceroy's House. Passing through the State Rooms we inadvertently walked in on the viceregal party at tea. We made a hasty withdrawal. Henry arranged a little dinner party for me with some grand members of His Excellency's staff as guests. One evening we went to HE's cinema, where General Wavell was in the audience. I went to dinner with Sir Kenneth Fitze, a doyen of the Indian Political Service and father of my friend Sam, who was just about to come out as an IA cadet. Uncle Henry arranged for me to attend the presentation in the Hall of Assembly of the National Budget for 1944. I was given the front seat in the Viceroy's Box. The attendance of members was very sparse, almost limited to Europeans and the Muslim League representatives. Members from the Congress Party having refused to endorse India's support of the war had boycotted the Assembly. Some of them had been locked up for active participation in the Civil Disobedience of 1942.

The budget presentation was made by Jeremy Raisman (ICS) as Finance Member of the Government. I met him in England over forty years later as a friend and neighbour of John West, shortly before John succeeded me as Chairman of Salvesen.

I boldly asked Uncle Henry one day if I might borrow his car to drive round Delhi. He agreed without hesitation. His machine was a magnificent powerful La Salle coupe of 1933, with a dickey. It had been commissioned by a Native

State Maharajah and a few years later passed on to Henry at a fraction of its original price. I nervously piloted it down the avenues of New Delhi and through the great Indian Gate with its memorial to the Indian dead of the Great War. At one stage I was stopped by a hefty policeman who wanted to fine me for not observing a crossing. He forgave me as an army man on leave.

At Uncle Henry's hospitable table I was surprised to find that he used a tooth pick, evidently habitual for Europeans in India. I had been brought up to hold that tooth picks were socially unacceptable. Years later I dropped my prejudice and adopted that healthy practice.

My second leave was also in Delhi with my friend Cliff Pinfold. By then Uncle Henry had on the retirement of Lord Linlithgow as Viceroy moved to Quetta as Chief Medical Officer in Baluchistan. We stayed at the Imperial Hotel, second only to Maidens. We explored thoroughly the mosques and monuments of Delhi, followed by a trip to Agra. On the way there we stopped for two nights at Khurja, where my father's sister Mary was a missionary of the Church of Scotland.

Aunt Mary came to meet us at Khurja station, not far from Delhi. There was great excitement as we stepped out on the platform. People seemed never to have seen a European before and fingered us to make sure we were real. We climbed on to two tongas and followed a long dusty road to Khurja. On arrival at her house I prepared to pay off the tongas with a reasonable sum, say 2 rupees. 'No no' cried Aunt Mary 'I have never paid them more than 12 annas and that's quite enough!' So 12 annas it was, and they departed grumbling.

Aunt Mary had been a missionary in the area for over thirty years. She had been in Bulandshahr close by when news came of the outbreak of the Great War. When I asked her how many conversions to Christianity she had made, her answer was straight forward. Just two she said, one a girl she had rescued from the Bengal famine of 1942 and adopted. She was fully taken up with social work for families in Khurja and the villages round about. Aunt Mary had a pony trap of which she was very proud. One admirer had not long before given her two trotting bullocks to draw it. But Rose had been stolen and the second was not strong enough to draw the cart on its own. Aunt Mary must have had a lonely life in Bulandshahr and Khurja. When she retired she elected to stay in India and was placed in a mission house in Missourie. But her memory failed and she returned to Scotland to die. From Khurja Cliff and I went on to Agra for the Taj Mahal, always to be viewed by moonlight, the great fort and Sikander's tomb.

Early in 1944 I received an invitation inviting me to spend a weekend in Nathia Gali as a guest of Sir George Cunningham, The Governor of North West Frontier Province (NWFP), in his hot weather house. That was almost a royal command, which I gladly accepted. I took the bus to Nathia Gali, about 3,000ft higher. There was some snow from the winter and it rained most of the time I was there. Sir George must have met my mother when on leave at St Andrews and invited me for that. I saw little of their Excellencies except at meals. They left me in the care of their aide-de-camp (ADC) and we played hours of snooker.

Sir George as Governor of NWFP had a dominating status, reporting only to the Viceroy. Before independence and separation, three years later, he was asked by Jawahrlal Nehru to organise a meeting of tribal chiefs at a Jirgah, for Nehru to address them in favour of a United India. The assembly was a disaster. The tribal chiefs refused to consider any proposal with subordination of Muslims to Hindus. Nehru was furious with Sir George for failing to promote

the case for a unified civil state, but Sir George had consci-
entiously performed his duty. When the break was eventually
decided Sir George was asked to remain for a spell as Governor of Pakistan's NWFP and he took this on. Nehru was
leader of the Congress Party and destined to become the
first prime minister of independent India.

In autumn 1944 I was further invited for Christmas at
Government House in Peshawar. I was able to decline grace-
fully. I was to celebrate my 21st birthday on Christmas Eve
and there were other festivities planned. I met Sir George
again later in St Andrews and we chatted on our way to and
from golf.

The European war ended in May 1945 and was celebrated in Abbottabad with two days holiday and a grand
parade. We in India were all too conscious that for us it was
no more than the beginning of the end, with months and
years more of battles in the East to come before Japan was
defeated.

From March to August, training continued at full stretch
right up to the end of the Japanese war in August. I was more
than busy with supervising drills and range firing, extended
to include the invaluable Sten gun, preparing the weekly
programmes for my battalion, checking stores, the debugging
of charpoys (beds), which had to be regularly immersed in
hot water to clean them, and the chores of checking and
signing the individual sheets of my company. There was
plenty of time for games, in which we all took part. Volley-
ball was the great game, with numbers usually limited to six
a side. Indian players showed themselves far better than their
British counterparts. There were also regular sports compe-
titions at battalion and occasionally Centre level. Cliff Pinfold
distinguished himself in welterweight boxing. The Jawans
also laid on concerts in the batallian, which we had to attend.
There seemed to be interminable dancing and songs accom-

panied by single notes from hand pumped organs.

Early in 1945 news came that Pat Bourne of 6th Gurkhas had been killed in Burma. I had met him first on the D & M Course at Arangaon. Back in Abbottabad he entertained me at dances (nach) in the 6th Gurkhas Centre, where reluctant Gurkhas performed as dancing girls and rakshi, the local spirit, was generously supplied. Pat Bourne's father lived in Oxford. I tried to contact him after the war but failed to find him.

I felt that I had been long enough at the Centre and was ready to move to an active battalion, preferably 5/13, favoured by Peter Lugg. But this was overtaken by a new scheme providing for early release of university scholars to start their studies. I put in for that, as did my cousin Ken Clarence Smith. It should have come through in time for the autumn term at Oxford, but somewhere there was an administrative failure. That was kindly corrected by Ken, who went to the India Office on my behalf, but my release did not come through till February 1946 when I flew home in time to start at New College, Oxford, in April 1946.

PART III

Envoi

The Japanese War came to an end in August 1945 with the atomic bomb and Hiroshima. It was an immense relief. Having heard the news by radio I went to a section of recruits on parade and told them, to their great joy. No more fighting; we could all go home to our families. Although there was some dismay at the atomic bomb, most of us, in India as in Europe, welcomed it, realising that we would otherwise have been condemned to a lengthy further struggle, with thousands more killed on the way to Japan. We celebrated VJ day very quietly, thanking whatever God there be for our salvation.

The end of the war against Japan brought about an immediate and total run-down of the army. We had some months previously consulted our men on whether they wanted immediate release or a year's training first; the repetition of the question brought opposite answers. Regardless of preferences all were discharged. I was kept busy supervising the close down and pay offs of my No. 8 Company. Soon there was nothing more left for me to do than cutting and dispersing medal ribbons to our departing soldiers. As British in the Indian Army we were disappointed that we did not qualify for the Indian service medal but were treated for war decorations as members of the British Army.

Towards the end of the European war, or perhaps just after that, a group of four or five Afghan officers came down to Abbottabad for training. They turned up in our mess unheralded one evening after dinner where a few of us were reading or playing bridge. I got up to greet their leader and quickly found they knew almost no English. However I dredged up my past French and found that the leader had been educated at a French convent school in Kabul. They were not allowed to wear uniform so appeared in what seemed to us curious rigs of Norfolk jackets and knicker-bockers. They stayed being trained for two to three months and I became quite friendly with their leader during that period.

The war end left us a sober enough bunch most days in the mess, though there were periods of riotous parties, particularly when friends passed through from active units. To anyone of years and sense our parties must have seemed particularly silly, always ending in the same round of dirty songs. At one period I was drunk regularly every Saturday night. Some nights (this, I think, after the end of the war) we formed up and marched down the hill into another regiment's mess and out again. On guest night drinking was tempered by ceremonial. We toasted the King Emperor while the drum and fife band played 'God Save the King' outside. Towards the end of my time I started meeting one or two girls, nurses from the hospital, and there were dances at the Abbottabad Club or at Kakul. I was growing up.

In 1945 I started to learn the bagpipes. I introduced myself to the havildar who was training a pipe band from the Boys Company, and he gave me a weekly lesson. I used to go down to his cabin in the Lines and we would play and gossip while a comely Khattak lad with bobbed hair filled his hubble-bubble and offered me pilao. I blush now to think of Arab Gul's generosity to me and the little return I gave him. He wanted to be a jemadar and I spoke for him in the best quarters, but to no effect. I never became competent to do more than blow the first four bars of 'Highland Laddie' at bottle parties. Perhaps this was why I was too miserly to buy a proper set of pipes, but got a 'desi' set from the bazaar, made of light wood. The previous owner had filled the bag with gur (sugar) to make it soft, and chunks kept coming loose and gumming up the operations. There was also trouble with the air valve, which was not as non-return as it should be.

With my release pending and my company dissolved I was glad to take some annual leave. Three of us drove up to the hills, past Muzaffarabad and down into Srinagar in the Vale of Kashmir where we hired a traditional houseboat, admirably serviced by the owner. We amused ourselves swimming and boating in the Dal Lake, playing tennis and visiting the town. We called in at the Club; with the season ending, it was almost deserted. Two years later, in defiance of the independence settlements, gangs of tribesmen occupied Muzaffarabad and tried to take over all Kashmir. They were disowned by the new Pakistan Government and repelled by Indian troops from Kashmir but established new frontiers within the Kashmir borders. This situation remains in 2013.

One day I was called in by the adjutant and detailed to look after an officer, Colin Oliff, in close arrest on his way to Court Martial in Rawlpindi. I had known him slightly in D Bn two years earlier. Colin told me that he was so disgusted with the atomic bombs that he decided to desert. He had been quickly picked up by the MPs and put in my care. He declared no intention to escape but for security I slept on a bed close to his with the room key on my wrist. Four or five years later, when I was deep into whaling, we had a letter from his father. Colin had not settled down on his return to England and could we give him a job as a whaler? Harold agreed that we could not help. The risk of collapse on the whaling grounds was too much.

In November I heard from Kennedy McWhirter that our close friend Sam Fitze had died in Kuala Lumpur, supposedly in a sports accident. It was only after my return to England that his mother told me that he had shot himself. He had served with 19th Lancers in Burma in the last campaign. When the regiment moved to Malaya he was posted as ADC to the divisional commander. Finding he could not cope with the job he returned to the regiment. In a fit of depression he blew out his brains. No one could have predicted this.

The easing of fuel restrictions after the war made it possible for Jimmy Gregory, the Centre Motor Transport Officer (MTO) to take some of us out to visit the remains of the Greek town of Taxila, founded by Alexander the Great, not very far away. We called at Hassan Abdul, with its Sikh shrine and lake, soon to be virtually closed with the establishment of Pakistan and the departure of its Sikh population.

My release came through in early February with instructions to proceed to Karachi for transport home in a Dakota. No luggage but a small overnight bag was to be taken. I had accumulated quite a quantity of kit during my three years in India and a number of books. I packed it all into my tin trunk and other suitcases, including my precious violin. Arriving at Karachi I could find no place to register my luggage. So I just left it on the platform, fully addressed and labelled to my home, in the hope that it would get back sometime. And it did arrive safely in May or June.

The trip home involved a first hop to Palestine, then to Tripoli and finally an airfield outside Cambridge. We were kept going during the flight by K rations. The bomb bays of the Dakota had very little leg room but what did that matter. We were going home. Thousands thankfully took the same route.

I started as an undergraduate at New College, Oxford, in the summer of 1946 and graduated in 1948. While at Oxford I became attached to a fellow student, Margaret Whale; we married in 1950. We have been blessed with three children and nine grandchildren.

I expected on leaving India in 1946 that I would never return. Air transport was expensive, and I would have no reason to go back. This held until the early 1970s when my company, attracted by the opportunities arising in the North Sea oil industry, commissioned a floating drill ship. I went to New Delhi in 1973 to fix a contract for the ship and took the opportunity to look for contacts in the Indian Army, formed on independence in July 1947. Working as our agents in Delhi were VK Malhotra and Kailash Seigal. 'Malu' Malhotra had been in 8/13 during my time; Kailash Seigal, a brother in law of Malhotra, had had a period of service with the new Indian Army before becoming a ship broker. Their firm helped us in our drill ship negotiations and we became good friends.

The several business visits at that time led us to tourist trips, and we had many up to 2012, when we declared an end to long-distance travel in the infirmity of old age. Our trips, always in winter, covered most of India, including Assam, Calcutta and North Bengal. In the south we took in Tamil Nadu and Kerala. We visited the great lake and dam of Periyar, built in the early 1900s, a magnificent feat of British and Indian engineering. This was well celebrated by Maud Diver with an article in a *Blackwoods Magazine* issue of 1942.

We have been to Pakistan twice since the war. In 1982 we included in our tour of Rawlpindi, Peshawar and Lahore a visit to Abbottabad, now an important national centre for military training. We enjoyed the hospitality of Gohar Ayub and his family. Gohar, a son of General Ayub Khan, the former dictator, had been debarred from public life by the current dictator, Ziaul Haq (later killed in an air crash). After the establishment of Pakistan the FF Rifles had been absorbed into the Frontier Force Regiment (FFR). Our centre had become the home of the Baluch Regiment. The FFR had moved to the old 6th Gurkhas Centre close by. We were entertained by the FFR Centre Commander to coffee with some of his officers followed by lunch in their mess. Exploring on our own we walked down to the old D Bn Lines where I found my 8 coy office, hardly changed, and the bungalow which Bob Hargraves had rented. The corrugated pissoir near the entrance to the Lines was still in operation.

More recently, in 2007, we took part in a tour through Pakistan covering Karachi, Islamabad and Lahore. In Lahore we were invited to dinner by General Zahoor Malik. I had already met General Malik on his regular visits to Scotland from Lahore. Malik was like myself a 'Piffer' – an officer of a regiment traditionally part of the Panjab Frontier Force. The IA catchphrase was 'Once a Piffer, always a Piffer'. His dinner party enabled us to meet seven distinguished friends. Six were generals in the Pakistan Army; I had met one in Abbottabad. The seventh had been high in the Civil Service. The dinner was attended by only one wife, but we greatly enjoyed the company. Malik honoured us further by sending a fine album of photos taken on the occasion.

I have attended many Indian Army regimental and general reunions in England and continued contacts with personal friends, including Bob Hargraves and Hank Howlett, colleagues in Abbottabad. I saw little of Cliff Pinfold, my closest friend in Abbottabad. He decided to stay as a regular in the British Army, with periods of service in Germany. He retired as a Colonel and took a support job in the City. He married the girl next door in Beckenham, where they made their home.

I have maintained a strong interest in Indian history and literature. I have read most of what has been published since the war about the British in India. Biographies, memoirs, historic studies, novels all attest to the deep influence India has had on people of my generation who served there.

Kennedy McWhirter like myself returned early to take up his demyship at Merton College, Oxford. We were close together there. He was a teacher at Edmonton University in Canada for many years, later settling in Switzerland. He died rather early from a stroke.

My friendship with Harold Holloway resumed at Oxford when he came back to Exeter College. He had been captured by India. After graduating in law he went on to pursue a career as a lawyer there, based in Calcutta. He never married but he had a small loyal staff whom he rewarded by setting up with land. Having lost touch for thirty years we renewed our friendship at Kennedy McWhirter's funeral. Shortly afterwards he retired from India. I stayed with him at his country house in Sussex and admired the billiard table and benches from the Bengal Club which he had bought and set up. He took me, in an elderly Rolls-Royce driven by his Indian servant, to Batelaws, Rudyard Kipling's house in Sussex. There we admired the decorations designed by Rudyard's father Lockwood after his retiral from curatorship of the Lahore Museum. Harold died not long afterwards, having never previously consulted a doctor. In his work, extending to Pakistan and Bangladesh, he had specialised in advising ex-rulers of the Native States. Through that he acquired a considerable collection of ornaments and art works from the British period. He was also one of the earliest members of the British Association for Cemeteries in South Asia (BACSA). He enrolled me as a life member before I heard of its existence and without telling me. I have had no kinsmen buried in India, but have found BACSA interesting from its work in India and sometimes useful as a seller of Indian books.

Looking back at that period I am astonished how well the war behaved for me. Apart from the perils of active service, which was kept outside my experience, the individual caught up in war usually at some point finds himself in the grip of hostile circumstances which he cannot control – intolerable superiors, physical discomfort, boredom, frustration. I suffered none of these. My Indian Army dreams were never spoilt. I was devoted to my regiment, got on well with my commanders, lived in a mild climate, and had a job of absorbing interest which kept me busy and happy.